Dealing with that Other God

By Bob Mumford

LIFECHANGERS ®

P.O. Box 3709 ❖ Cookeville, TN 38502
931.520.3730 ❖ lc@lifechangers.org

PLUMBLINE

Published by:

LIFECHANGERS ®
L I B R A R Y   S E R I E S

P.O. Box 3709 | Cookeville, TN 38502
(800) 521-5676 | www.lifechangers.org

Dealing with that Other God

By Bob Mumford

A little after midnight the doors of the emergency room opened and a tall, Afro-American gentleman was wheeled in on a gurney. He was rail thin, unkempt, and in the process of dying. It was 1963. Judith and I had just finished training to be medical missionaries, and I was working as a medical technician in the Atlantic City Hospital to keep our bills paid. Working the midnight to 7:00 AM shift was miserable. This poor gentleman had lived in poverty, a shack at the Atlantic City dump. The skin on the bottom of his feet must have been a quarter-inch thick because it had been years since he had owned a pair of shoes. He was one of the most pathetic, yet majestic, human beings I had ever encountered. Inside, dwelled a man. We are born, male or female, into poverty or prosperity. We have to *choose* to become a true man or woman.

As I prepared minor comforts for him, the Lord filled me with an overwhelming sense of compassion. As we talked, I shared the Lord with him, discovering he was quite a strong a believer in Jesus Christ as Lord. We prayed together and talked about the Lord for some time. About 4:00 AM he silently passed into the presence of the Lord. Wheeling him down to the morgue, it seemed difficult to say goodbye.

About one hour later, around 5:00 AM, they brought into emergency a wealthy homeowners from Ventnor City, a more exclusive part of Atlantic City. This man of middle-eastern descent had fallen in the tub and struck the back of his head, proving to be fatal. Taking him down to the morgue, placing him side by side with the man from the dump, I was struck quite forcibly that death was the ultimate equalizer.

As I stood looking at both of them, the Lord said, "What do *you* see?" The man from the dump knew the Lord, filled with joy. My aunt, the night supervisor, knew the history and not-so-pleasant reputation of the second man. Without knowing it, the Lord was preparing me for future years of ministry. I am still deeply affected by this powerful experience. My sense was that I was actually living the parable of Lazarus and the rich man[1]. Somehow, the "equalizer" lesson provided me a deep and lasting freedom from materialism, pressing for that which is eternal as compared to all that is temporary and fleeting.

This does not imply impoverishment or destitution as a prerequisite to enter the Kingdom of God; however, it does establish our Kingdom value system. In this *Plumbline* I am seeking to explore and unfold with you "that other god." Its name is mammon. Jesus identified it in His sermon on the mount when he said, "No one can serve two masters; for either he will hate the one and love the other, or else he will be loyal to the one and despise the other.

---

1   Luke 16:19-31

You cannot serve God and mammon."[2] Mammon comes from an Aramaic (the language Jesus spoke) word, *mamonas*, which means wealth or riches. Two things are most important to note in Jesus' statement. First, Jesus personifies mammon making it equal with God as to its potential of strength of influence on our lives. Second, you can only serve and be ruled by one god at a time; the governing influence of one negates the influence of the other. According to Jesus you must make a choice of which one will be your decisive master. This lesson seems to have been literally "written on the tablets of my heart."

As we proceed through this *Plumbline* I would sincerely ask each of you to do a careful self-evaluation of YOU. Please do not use these biblical insights to evaluate others in your world. Mammon is surrounded and masked by a host of illusions that promise much but deliver little leading to disillusionment. It is my prayer that through this *Plumbline* we may help you to recognize and begin to come to a Kingdom freedom that is fully able to deliver what it has promised. This is a most urgent issue. Let's have the courage to allow Him to speak.

Everywhere all the time

In our culture money is ubiquitous. Something that is ubiquitous is *"existing or being everywhere at the same time: constantly encountered"*[3]. Ubiquitous is

---

2 Matt 6:24 NKJV
3 Merriam-Webster

also a description of God. God is everywhere, but He is not only ubiquitous. He is omnipresent. Money is not God, but it permeates society to a depth almost like one. Money, while limited in its effect, still exhibits a profound influence. It isn't omnipresent, but it is ubiquitous: everywhere, speaking to and seeking to rule everyone about everything. Listen to the phrase: "follow the money." While preparing for a delayed surgical procedure, the technician assured the patient, "Do not worry, the procedure will happen. It is all about money!"

Mysterious or overt, the presence or absence of money influences or controls most decisions in our personal lives. Think about your life decisions, small and large: the home you live in; the car you drive; if and where you will go on vacation; the quality of your health care; if, when, and how you will retire and the quality of life you will enjoy when you do. We live in a materialistic culture of money and possessions. It has become the ultimate value system displacing or over-shadowing those values that have historically been the foundation of healthy societies, sound institutions, and beneficent governments.

The Genesis of Mammon

Mammon is empowered by the corruption released in humanity through Adam's fall. God had warned Adam that in the day he ate the fruit of the tree of knowledge that "dying you will die" [Literal Hebrew]. I believe God's pronouncement defines the very essence of corruption. I earnestly desire for each of you to grasp the full depth and power of corruption because it is the driving dynamic in our increasingly chaotic and violent world. Allow me to give you some definitions from the Merriam-Webster Dictionary:

a: *dishonest or illegal behavior especially by powerful people (such as government officials or police officers)*

b: *inducement to wrong by improper or unlawful means (such as bribery) the corruption of government officials*

c: *a departure from the original or from what is pure or correct [Underline mine]*

In the New Testament the Greek word for corruption, *phthora,* signifies a bringing or being brought into an inferior or worse condition, a destruction or corruption.[4] When the first pair fell into corruption, not only was humanity infected but all creation over which they had been given dominion.[5] The corruption released on mankind was so inexorable and destructive that in a mere nine generations after Adam, humanity had morally decayed to the point where God was ready to destroy everything and everyone!

---

4   Vine's Expository Dictionary of Biblical Words, Copyright © 1985, Thomas Nelson Publishers.

5   See Romans 8:20-22.

Now the earth was <u>corrupt</u> in the sight of God, and the earth was filled with violence. God looked on the earth, and behold, it was <u>corrupt</u>; for all flesh had <u>corrupted</u> their way upon the earth [Underline mine] (Gen. 6:11-12).

The end of all flesh has come before Me; for the earth is filled with violence because of them; and behold, I am about to destroy them with the earth (Gen. 6:13).

With the fall everyone, none excluded, was made subject to the fallen mindset, and we all became takers. Created in the image of the consummate Giver, now that image has been corrupted. God the Father, who is the consummate Giver, must be reconciled with the consummate takers. That is the spiritual warfare involved in our personal journey of redemption. We are each born with natural desires, which left ungoverned, will cause us to be disqualified from walking in the freedom of the Kingdom of God. Eve saw "that the tree was desirable"; she failed to *govern* her desire to be like God leading to the corruption of our entire race and empowering the god of mammon ever since.

Ungoverned desire, driven by eros, is a self-referential love that does not seek to give to the object of love but rather to take from it to satisfy personal desires. Ungoverned desire has corrupted societies throughout human history. In every strata of society we see "a departure from the original or from what is pure or correct": corruption of individuals, families, corporations, and institutions. In the political and business community, foundational morals and ethics are increasingly corrupted or abandoned entirely. Hollywood, the media, the educational system, and elected officials embrace and promote corruption in various forms. The advertising and marketing industry has become predatory, appealing to every fleshly desire imaginable. As I was preparing for this *Plumbline* I felt overwhelmed and urgent; when you see the depth of it, it is nauseous and repulsive.

The Departure

Throughout my journey I have been tempted repeatedly to "serve that other god," using the ministry as a means of financial gain and personal advancement or aggrandizement. Over the decades I have watched scores of anointed men and women become disqualified and ruined, losing their spiritual credibility and effectiveness in the cause of Christ because the desire for mammon captured and imprisoned them. Lest I be misunderstood, I do not believe nor do I think Scripture teaches that money or wealth is wrong or evil. Wealth empowers us to do tremendous good and advance the purposes of the Kingdom. As Paul wrote to Timothy, it is not money but "the <u>love</u> of money" that is the root of evil[6]. *The Message* paraphrases of this verse in a manner that is most compelling.

---

6   1 Timothy 6:10

Lust [ungoverned desire] *for money brings trouble and nothing but trouble. Going down that path, some lose their footing in the faith completely and live to regret it bitterly ever after (1 Timothy 6:10).*

God intends mammon to serve God's people and purposes, not the other way around. In Luke 16:9-13, Jesus told His followers that the wise use of "unrighteous mammon" would have eternal benefits. Furthermore, He added that the measure of their faithfulness in the use of worldly wealth would be the measure for their ability to be entrusted with greater responsibility. Picture yourself being handed a case of dynamite. Mishandle it and it can destroy you and everyone close to it. If you handle it wisely and cautiously it can move a mountain. We believe in prosperity, but we must worship the God who gives prosperity, not the prosperity He gives us.

Open Doors

Mammon doesn't just knock at your door and announce, "Hi, Bob. I'm here to enslave you and ruin your life." Like a practiced salesperson he first lays out the bait. "Bob, I'd like to take just a moment of your time, and let me show you what I can do for you. Would you like to have all your needs and wants comfortably met? Don't you wish to provide for all the missionaries drilling new wells in Africa and help take care of Widow Simmons from the church who is trying to survive on her monthly Social Security check? It could be yours for the taking."

As amusing as this story may seem, we need to seriously examine the progression of events that seeks to open doors for that other god. Allow me to begin with a passage from James which clearly lays out the dynamic that is at work. I will adapt the application slightly to fit within our context.

> *Let no one say when he is tempted, "I am being tempted by God"; for God cannot be tempted by evil, and He Himself does not tempt anyone. But each one is tempted when he is carried away and enticed by his own lust. Then when lust has conceived, it gives birth to sin; and when sin is accomplished, it brings forth death (James 1:13-15).*

Within us all are desires, some of which are very human and legitimate; e.g. security, belonging, being loved, satisfaction of basic life needs, and a sense of purpose for life. Other desires originate in the depth of eros: prestige, power, control, unlimited pleasure, etc. Satan appealed to both types of desires in Jesus' temptation. The fulfillment of Jesus' desires was there for the taking if Jesus would just reach for it. However, Jesus chose to govern His desires by submitting them to the principles of the Kingdom. "It is written . . . it is written . . . it is written."

Please follow carefully the progression from James:

First, desires which remain ungoverned may increase in strength, almost taking on a life of their own, becoming lust. "Lust" is the Greek word, *epithuma,* which is used thirty-nine times in the New Testament and means strong desire, craving, or longing. It may be used of longings for things that are good or bad but is primarily used to describe things which are forbidden[7]. Paul tells us that if we begin to obey our lusts—strong desires, cravings, longings—then we are allowing sin to take control and reign in our mortal bodies.[8]

Second, when we give place to lust, it releases a malignant energy that is "conceived" (or "takes hold") in our persons. Gradually a force comes forth that endeavors to divert us from our intended journey with Jesus causing us to all too frequently "miss the mark" to which we have been called.

Finally, when sin has reached complete maturity it begins to produce death in us. This seems to be some form of physical, spiritual, and eternal death infecting areas of our life separated from the grace of God, no longer subject to the life and conviction of the Holy Spirit or obedient to the Word of God. At this point corruption has begun to set in bringing the possibility of spreading death to the rest of our beings. Picture a member of your body that has been cut off from its life-giving flow of blood or has been injured or diseased in some manner causing it to die. It begins

---

7   *Thayer's Greek Lexicon.* Strong's NT number 1939.
8   See Romans 6:12.

to decompose (corrupt), and if not removed it may become gangrenous. Spiritually, if corruption in an area of my life is not identified, it becomes an open door for a ruling spiritual force to possess and enslave that portion of my being. I believe this is what Jesus was referring to when He personified mammon—He was actually referring to a *spiritual being* who is capable of governing and controlling my life. Carefully note the difference between God and mammon: God gives us freedom resulting in life; mammon enslaves, resulting in death.

Listen to Paul's warning to Timothy, his son in the faith:

> *But those who want to get rich fall into temptation and <u>a snare</u> and many foolish and harmful desires which plunge men into ruin and destruction. <u>For the love of money is a root of all sorts of evil</u>, and some by longing for it have wandered away from the faith and pierced themselves with many griefs [Underline mine] (1 Tim 6:9-10).*

When Mammon gains its foothold in a man or woman, he brings a troop of associates who carry in their own varieties of complication and corruption. As we progress through this list let us be ruthless in self-evaluation asking the Lord to shine the light of His Spirit deep into our souls. We seek diagnostic truth not introspection, condemnation, or guilt. The Spirit of the Lord brings joy and freedom.

I. The Fallen Mindset

Having received the fallen mindset Adam and Eve ceased being God conscious and became self-conscious. Perhaps it could be more accurate to say that they became *self-focused*. Eros governs the fallen mindset and it gives birth to a number of different motivations that serve to drive us further into the arms of mammon. You know my lists and here it is:

Anxiety and Fear.

The first words man uttered after the fall were, "I was afraid,"[9] and fear has been a driving force in human history ever since. Which one of us does not battle fear in some form on a daily basis. When Jesus called out the other god in Matthew 6:24, he immediately followed with these words, "Therefore I say to you, do not be anxious." He then instructs his followers not to be anxious for three basic needs: food, drink, and clothing. In our modern western society we do not often consider these as things we would be concerned about, but in Jesus' day any one of these could be imminently threatened very quickly. In a modern context we might relate more if Jesus had said, "Don't be anxious about paying your bills, keeping your job, affording your health insurance, or how you will live in your old age." Today these can be

9   Genesis 3:10

most pressing issues that raise our anxiety levels and disrupt our sleep.

Unfortunately the King James Bible has translated Jesus' words, "Take no thought for your life," which has caused some "hyper-spiritual" people to believe wise forethought in planning, saving, and making provision for future needs is in some strange manner a lack of true faith. Quite the contrary, Jesus commanded His followers to make use of "the wealth [*mammon*] of righteousness"[10] to provide for their future. Solomon warned that as a result of failure to provide for coming needs, "Poverty will come on you like a bandit and scarcity like an armed man."[11] Planning for the future is an imminent responsibility. Men who think life insurance a waste of money may be failing to foresee for their family's future thus inviting poverty and need for those they leave behind. Parents who die without having executed a will detailing the disposition of their estate leave an open door for greed to destroy their family. Siblings can be very loving until thousands of undesignated dollars are dropped on the table. Suddenly eros is inflamed, and an uncivilized war ensues, which can leave wounds and resentments that are difficult to heal.

Let's look carefully at what Jesus was saying. Matthew uses the Greek word *merimna,* which means "to be anxious; to be troubled with cares"[12] or "to

---

10   See Luke 16:9

11   Proverbs 6:11 (NIV)

12   Thayer's Greek Lexicon

care for, be anxious about, think earnestly upon, scan minutely."[13] There is a careful distinction between the occasional and transient concern verses the anxiety and fear that become a preoccupation or obsession dominating and controlling our motives, decisions, and our entire attitude toward our present and future lives. At this point we have begun to be influenced by the dominion of the other god. Men and women who have suffered catastrophic losses can be driven to suicide. Why? Their god has failed and to paraphrase Paul, they are "without hope and without [g]od in this world."[14] Fear can rarely be conquered directly; it must be overridden and displaced by faith.

Greed

Greed is driven by an ungoverned feeling that no matter how much you have, it is never enough—you must have more. Greed is something that Bill next door has, never me. But consider the fact that I may be quite happy with my $49 LG smart phone until Bill showed me what he could do with his $289 Galaxy. Then for about six months I am thrilled with my Galaxy until I'm sitting next to a business executive on the plane that is working off the latest iPhone. He begins to show me all its bells and whistles; it's slimmer, the display is amazing, and the camera takes pictures you could mount on your living room wall.

13   Liddell and Scott Abridged Greek Lexicon
14   Ephesians 2:12

"Greed" is never used in the King James Bibles where the Greek word is translated "covetousness." Almost all modern versions translate the Greek word as "greed" where it always means a desire to have more. Erich Fromm (1900-1980), a social psychologist, described greed as a bottomless pit that exhausts the person in an endless effort to satisfy the need without ever reaching satisfaction.[15] Fromm is describing the dynamic of the other god—he takes away and gives nothing of lasting value in return.

Paul warns about "greed, which amounts to idolatry[16]." Greed has become a moral norm in our culture, and we are a nation of idolaters. It is relentlessly fueled by the barrage of advertising on television and through the internet that is designed to produce a subtle dissatisfaction with who are we and what we possess. The incessant fog of the "lust of the flesh, the lust of the eyes, and the boastful pride of life"[17] endeavors to cloud our vision of all that is true, real, and has eternal value. Whatever allows me to feel good, look good, and makes me a feel a little better about myself is readily accepted. These are the snares of the other god.

Envy

In the simplest terms, envy is counting everyone else's blessings but not my own! Envy is the brother

15   From *Wikipedia*; "Greed".
16   Colossians 3:5
17   See 1 John 2:16

of greed albeit usually more subtle and hidden. Greed is clearly recognized and understood in our contemporary culture, but in recent years envy as a social dynamic has become less prominent in our thinking. Envy is given so little consideration today it will benefit us to examine this pervasive and powerful destructive force. As I have come to understand envy I would liken it to hypertension (high blood pressure). The medical community has labeled it "the silent killer" because an individual with high blood pressure is unaware of it even though he is at a higher risk of a stroke or heart attack. Likewise, envy is able to lie unnoticed in an individual or group of individuals, subtly but insidiously corrupting value judgments of self and others, crippling the ability to live by a Kingdom value system. The apostle Paul lists envy as a manifestation of the fallen mindset grouping it with the works of the flesh and the characteristics of a corrupt culture.[18]

Unlike greed, which desires to possess things, Envy is usually focused on another person or a group of people. If I envy another person, it is because he or she has something I believe I should or could possess. Wealth is not the only thing that can arouse envy; it may also be incited by privilege, position, natural talents, or simple "good luck." Envy can be singular, focused on a particular individual or group or a generalized attitude that looks at self or circumstance

18   See Romans 1:29; Galatians 5:21; 1 Timothy 6:4; and, Titus 3:3.

and feels in some way cheated by life because we are not as prosperous, gifted, fortunate, attractive, or blessed as those around us.

Envy carries with it the possibility of being a destructive force—it is a spiritual dynamic which can be directed at another person. In many cultures envy is identified with the "evil eye" and is associated with witchcraft, the power to inflict harm through magic, curses, and spells. In his classic work, *Envy*, sociologist Helmut Schoeck, writes:

> *From time immemorial suspicion of witchcraft or black magic has fallen upon those who have had cause to be envious—of someone less ugly than themselves, of lucky parents, or the peasant with a good harvest and healthy cattle, etc.*[19]

In Mark 7:22, the Gospel records that Jesus listed the "evil eye" (Literal Greek) as one of the attitudes emanating out from a man or woman's inner being that may defile them. Modern translations uniformly translate these words as "envy." We should note that Jesus also refers to the eye in a similar manner in the middle of his discourse on wealth in Matthew 6:22. Here He says that a good eye, one that is clear, without mixture, and healthy, will fill our whole person with light. However, He also warned that an eye that is evil (bad, harmful, malicious, or wicked) will fill us

19   Helmut Schoeck, *Envy: A Theory of Social Behavior;* © 1966 by Helmut Schoeck. P. 40.

with darkness. I understand the eyes to represent the attitude with which we view others, circumstances, and the world around us. If our vision is colored with greed or envy then we have filled ourselves with a darkness that will affect every area of our lives. This "great" darkness defiles us jeopardizing our inheritance in the Kingdom of God.

Concerning envy, Schoeck writes:

Envy is always between neighbors [individuals or groups with whom we have reason to be in contact]. *It is not the absolute differences between men which feed envy, but subjective perception, the* <u>*optics of envy.*</u> *In other words, the envious man* <u>*sees*</u> *what confirms his envy.*

Envy is a very early, inescapable, and unappeasable drive in man, which induces the envious man constantly to react to his environment in such a way that his envy cannot be assuaged.[20] [Underline mine]

In a larger context Schoeck has very accurately described mammon and its ubiquitous power to infiltrate, influence, and dominate individuals or an entire culture. Envy is the root of the entitlement mentality that is eating away at the heart of the work ethic. It opens the door to demanded socialism, which has proved a failure in every nation that has tried it.

20   Schoeck, 27

Greed and envy infect a culture producing a social malaise that has been labeled "affluenza."

Affluenza

Affluenza is a term coined late in the last century to describe "a painful, contagious, socially transmitted condition of overload, debt, anxiety, and waste resulting from the dogged pursuit of more.[21]" Affluenza exists as a result of "excessive consumerism" and is credited with contributing to increase in mental illness, amplifying the economic gap between rich and poor, and a general unhappiness of the members of a society. The "dark eye" of affluenza had taken hold in the church in Laodicea causing them to become lukewarm in their affection for the Lord who declared to them, "Because you say, 'I am rich, and have become wealthy, and have need of nothing, and you do not know that you are wretched and miserable and poor and blind and naked.'"[22] It is my deep personal conviction that much of the church, in America and indeed most of the western world, has been infected with and is being consumed by this disease to which it is almost totally blind. As a result most of its power and voice has been compromised.

Prosperity and material increase are neither wrong nor inherently evil, but when they are presented as absolutes in the context of the gospel they provide a false center that dilutes our devotion to the person of

21   See "Affluenza," from Wikipedia.
22   Revelation 3:17

Jesus and keeps us from embracing the full experience of what it means to journey with Jesus in the walk of faith. Remember the words of Paul to Timothy that those infected with affluenza, "have wandered away from the faith and pierced themselves with many griefs."[23] We compromise with greed and envy to our spiritual peril.

II. The Diagnostic

In my training to become a medical missionary, the doctor who was training me relentlessly pounded into me this principle of diagnostics: *Don't just treat the symptoms; look for the root cause of the symptoms and treat that.* Permit me to present to you seven diagnostic "symptoms" that may uncover for you the presence of the influence of "the other god" or one of his lieutenants working in your life. As I do so, please do not allow yourself to fall prey to morbid self-condemnation; present yourself to the Holy Spirit, asking Him to lead you carefully in this self-evaluation. Recognize the symptoms and take the medicine!

1. Incessant Anxiety

Managing our finances wisely is critical to walking in the Kingdom as is witnessed by the emphasis on it in the parables and teachings of Jesus. However, if money and possessions become a preoccupation or

---

23   1 Timothy 6:10

"false center," they have taken an illegal priority in our lives. Like a pebble in a shoe, this anxiety is not necessarily debilitating, but it is always there drawing our attention away thus throwing life out of balance. As I have previously stated, the transient anxiety or concern provoked by financial crisis is normal; however, if it is incessant then there is cause for concern. Suffering an occasional headache is normal, but if it persists for an extending period of time it merits a visit to a doctor to determine the underlying cause.

2. Future Fear

Future fear was a condition that Jesus was addressing in His sermon on the mount. In speaking to His followers He told them their anxiety was expressed when they said, "What will we . . . what will we . . . what will we?" It was not concern about any particular present need but specifically fear and worry concerning what future circumstances might threaten their provision for life. How often have you found yourself saying, "How will I ever afford to . . . ?," "Will there be enough . . . ?," or, "What will happen if . . . ?" We live anticipating that someplace down the road a bogey man of some kind is going to jump out of a tree and devour our 401(k), our health, or the national economy.

Remember Y2K? Because of a possible glitch in computer software, multitudes of people withdrew huge amounts of cash, stocked up on food, bought generators and weapons anticipating the social apocalypse that would follow the failure of the world's computer systems. At 12:01 AM on January 1, 2000, not a light blinked and no airplanes fell out of the sky. In the late 1970s hundreds of people bought large stockpiles of long term storage food because certain pundits predicted that the national economy would soon collapse engendering want and hunger. The hordes of food are now long outdated. Beware of any financial plan that appeals to fear.

Again, faith in God's provision for the future in no way negates or releases us from the responsibility of planning and providing for future needs. However, if we are not able to return to a place of rest in our hearts knowing Father sees and makes a way in every circumstance then we may be in some manner giving place to mammon becoming our source and security. Faith and faithfulness, not fear, must direct our financial management.

3. The Danger of Discontentment.

Being discontented has little or nothing to do with our circumstances. I have come to believe that it is a pervasive soulish state of being into which we may fall because of a fallen mindset. It is the root of greed and envy. Adam and Eve were quite contented until the serpent suggested that they did not have enough—there was something more and better that could be theirs if they would just reach out and take it. Undoubtedly they had seen the tree many times; however, now it was "good," "a delight," and "desirable." The seed of discontent, which had been sown in their hearts, now changed the appearance of the fruit of the tree, and it was something they "needed."

Discontentment focuses on unmet needs whether real or perceived. I was very content with my LG smart phone from Wal-Mart until Bill showed me his Samsung Galaxy! Suddenly I *needed* a Galaxy to do all the things I never knew I needed to do. Being discontented arises from an internal sense of need and want that can never be satisfied. No matter how many tools I have, I need the new model because it runs faster, is lighter, and has more attachments. The sense of discontent opens the door to compulsive buying, overspending, and excessive debt.

The needs Jesus mentioned in His sermon—food, drink, and clothing—*are* genuine needs; the issue was priorities of needs. The most pressing need of His followers was to lay hold of the Kingdom and a right understanding of the Father. If they did this, then other needs could be handled without falling prey to the snares of the fallen mindset.

Solomon summed it up perfectly when he wrote: "*The righteous has enough to satisfy his appetite, But the stomach of the wicked is in need*"[24]

The only antidote for discontentment is to cultivate contentment.

---

24   Proverbs 13:25

4. Skewed Value System

A skewed value system seeks to measure everything and everyone by how much it costs or the price of the things they have. Somehow we subtly think the bank president is a person of more worth than the bag lady on the street corner. It was this skewed thinking that James warned about when he wrote:

> For if a man comes into your assembly with a gold ring and dressed in fine clothes, and there also comes in a poor man in dirty clothes, and you pay special attention to the one who is wearing the fine clothes, and say, "You sit here in a good place," and you say to the poor man, "You stand over there, or sit down by my footstool," have you not made distinctions among yourselves, and become judges with evil motives?[25]

Who among us cannot count ourselves guilty of this to some degree. We are too often concerned about what we might *receive* from interaction with someone, rather than what we can *give* to them by way of comfort or encouragement.

5. The Tight Fist

Tight-fisted people are often the object of humor or scorn. We are all familiar Ebenezer Scrooge from Charles Dickens' 1843 classic, *A Christmas Carol*.

---

25   James 2:2-4

Scrooge ruled his tiny accounting house with an iron fist (closed tightly around every shilling) and kept poor Bob Cratchit and his family in abject poverty. Most notably, Scrooge was angry, without compassion, joyless, and alone. Scrooge's confrontation with the three ghosts was a cold slap of reality about the true values of life and how poor he really was. Next time you view this movie please take careful note of how Scrooge's illusions about money were unmasked, and when he repents he was "born again" as a new man filled with generosity and joy.

Those who are afflicted with a stingy outlook on life can make life painful not only for themselves but those around them. Fortunately, very few people are as tight-fisted as Scrooge, but many people fail to live with an open hand and miss achieving the essence of the Gospel that proclaims God as the consummate Giver whom we are to emulate. When giving they focus on the cost, usually to the last penny, and wince ever so slightly when they see it deducted from the checking account. Parents remind their children how much it costs to provide them with guitar lessons, and when the wife brings home a new pair of slacks the first question out of the husband is, "And how much did those cost?" Many tight-fisted people become hoarders with a chronic fear of giving away or throwing out things because they might need them someday.

III. Breaking Free from the Other God

Breaking free from the dominion of mammon requires much more than learning a new way of handling our finances and possessions. We have been invited on a journey of discovery out of the world system. Success on this journey requires a total transformation into an entirely new way of living, a Kingdom value system in the midst of a materialistic and predatory society. In some consummate manner, it requires us to be set free from the fallen mindset.

It is Father's goal for each of us to become "temptation proof." If we are temptation proof when the desire comes to put something on a credit card rather than saving for it, to look at the pornographic web site, or tell a "little" lie to avoid embarrassment we can look temptation in the eye without flinching and declare, "You don't govern me; I have subjected myself to the King and His Kingdom." Please witness how Jesus handled temptation when it confronted Him in the wilderness. As I understand it, this is the final goal of Paul's message in Romans 5 – 8, in which he writes, "Sin shall not be master over you [as a result of ungoverned desires], for you are not under law but under grace."[26]

Please hear me when I say that when we fail (sin—meaning to miss the mark) *the main issue is not forgiveness.* The issue is learning to govern the desires that caused me to miss the mark. Allow me to be even bolder, forgiveness does not change us,

26 Romans 6:14

we just feel better about ourselves. We were forgiven from the foundation of the world, and it is a settled issue in God's mind. If we are continually focused on forgiveness we will continually be focused on law (from which sin derives its power). We are to be Father conscious, not sin conscious.

God forgave us from the foundation of the world through the death of Christ, not just for our sakes but for *His* sake, that He might be free to reconcile with His creation. To that end He sent Christ to become Jesus, the pattern Son, who overcame temptation and learned to obey and thus became our high priest.[27] He is now the leader[28] of our faith guiding us on our journey of discovering the Kingdom and our inheritance as sons and daughters. A most urgent issue required for walking with the Lord is to break ungoverned desires.[29]

Unlearning survival skills

Transformation also requires the unlearning of the "survival skills" we acquired to function and survive in a hostile and predatory society. As a youth of sixteen I was forced to learn street-smart survival skills to provide for myself and my three sisters after our parents' ugly divorce. I was working as an attendant at

---

27   Hebrews 5:8

28   See Hebrews 12:2; Greek, *archegon*

29   If you wish to understand this in more detail, I would suggest orderingthr *Plumbline*, "Surrendering Ungoverned Desires" from Lifechangers at www.lifechangers.org.

a Sonoco gas station in the days when the attendants wiped your wind shield, checked your oil, and made sure your tires were properly inflated. A job well done often resulted in a nice tip from the customer. I quickly learned to ingratiate myself to the customers, manipulating and maneuvering them for a bigger tip.

Most of us come to the Kingdom with a well-developed set of survival skills. They may not all be centered on finances, but we all had to learn to survive in our own private jungles. Pre-school was our first jungle, and we progressed through to high school with the jungle becoming ever more sophisticated and potentially damaging. We developed defensive or aggressive survival skills, and those who did not learn were wounded, sometimes fatally as witnessed by the mental health professionals and addiction recovery groups.

The adult world offered new jungles, the office, the work site, the PTA, with the church being one of the most difficult to survive. When we come to the Kingdom, however, we must begin to surrender those survival skills that hinder us from living like mature sons or daughters. We run, hide, shift blame, cut corners, tell half-truths, try to control circumstances and others, seek promotion, maneuver, stay defensive, manipulate, and compromise all to survive in the world of wolves.

Listen to Jesus' words to His disciples: "Behold, I send you out as sheep in the midst of wolves; so be shrewd as serpents and innocent as doves."[30] Please consider Jesus' implication: to follow me, you must become a sheep, and I will send you out to face your mortal enemy, the wolves. Sheep have only one survival skill—following and staying close to the shepherd. For me, letting go of my hard learned survival skills to become a sheep was an ultimate challenge.

The contrast in lifestyle was brought home to me one day when I stopped to help a lady standing next to her run-down Buick. When I approached her asking if she needed some help, she snapped rather coldly, "I don't need any help! I'm okay." I was somewhat taken aback by her bluntness until I realized she must be thinking I was a wolf on the prowl. I answered, "I'm really not trying to put the make on you. I just really want to help." She softened ever so slightly, "No. I'm just out of gas, and a tow truck is on the way." Noticing there was a gas station close by I said, "It looks like you can't afford gas much less a tow truck." I offered her a $20 bill and said, "Just take this twenty bucks and put some gas in your car to get home."

She looked at me for a moment and finally said, "Ok, Sir Galahad, but at least let me have you over and fix a meal for you."

"No," I said, "I appreciate it, but you don't need to do that. Just take the money and I'll be going." Finally she accepted the money.

I'm sure she thought I was from another planet. She was used to living with wolves, and she didn't know what to do with a sheep when she met one. She had probably never met a man who wasn't a taker in some form or another; therefore, when I stepped out of my car her well-honed survival skills automatically went into gear.

Shrewd Serpents

Becoming a sheep doesn't mean that we become dumb as a sheep because Jesus added that we were to be shrewd as serpents. Freedom from street skills, does not mean losing my street smarts. I have seen Christians fall for the stupidest money-making schemes most often with good intent to "provide money for the Kingdom." They were innocent as doves but also dumb as a doorpost. Jesus was street smart. The gospel tells us that Jesus would not entrust Himself to men because He knew all men and what is in man.[31]

For a number of years I taught the Kingdom to prisoners in San Quentin, which is one of toughest prisons in the nation, housing California's most hardened and violent criminals. When I started I asked the prison chaplain, "What can I do to avoid being taken in by these men?" Waiting for some sage advice, I was shocked when he said, "Nothing! They *will* take you, these men are pros!" These men had lived by finely tuned survival skills, and a tragic number returned to prison after their release because they had learned to be predatory wolves that could not change.

31   John 2:24

Seven Disciplines or perhaps: "Taking the Medicine"

Having seen the journey that is before us, allow me to suggest seven simple—I did not say easy—disciplines, which if undertaken urgently and seriously will begin to free you from the ubiquitous influence of mammon.

*1. **Cling passionately to the Person of Christ**.* Jesus said, "Above all else, stay close to me, and I'll provide everything you need." (Mumford translation of Matthew 6:33). When following Christ and pleasing the Father become the center of our affections and energies everything else falls into place.

*2. **Have faith in the Father's character**.* God is a good father! How often Jesus referenced the charter of His Father in practical terms: He numbers our hairs; He knows our needs before we ask; He looks out for sparrows; He gives what is good; He answers when we ask; He shows mercy; He desires us to share in His Kingdom; He gives only good; He is faithful to His word. How can we help but rest in the love of such a Father?

The accuser whispers to us that the Father is not concerned about our pain; He will bless others before us; He is giving us what we deserve; and He is quick to punish His children. What a different Father than the One Jesus revealed! If we cannot establish an anchor of trust in the character of the Father then we face a difficult journey. Jesus made it clear that faith in the Father's care is the spiritual dynamic that will silence the voice of fear and anxiety. Mental gymnastics and positive confessions alone are most often impotent in this struggle. Our faith brings the eternal into our reality and empowers the Father to move on our behalf.

*3. **Immerse yourself in thankfulness**.* I believe other than love and faith, thankfulness is probably the attitude that most pleases the Father. It is most telling that in Paul's digression of corrupting humanity in Romans 1 that the first step away from God is the failure to honor Him and give thanks.[32] Failure to offer thanks demonstrates that we do not understand that God is THE GIVER. The psalmist declares that the one who offers a sacrifice of thanksgiving honors God[33] and rightly relates us to God as our source.

Thankfulness is the greatest antidote to greed, envy, discontentment, grumbling, and complaining. Recently I was walking up to my car, which is quite adequate, and the Lord said to me, "You are a wealthy man!" I burst into tears as I realized that I have more than the vast majority of the world and one-third of that world lives on less than $2 a day. I responded, "Thank you, Lord! Thank you for my car, thank you for my house with its bathroom that needs to be remodeled, thank you that I have a bathroom—I *am* a wealthy man!" The next time you feel deprived or lacking in some way begin to give thanks. Thank God you have eyes, you can walk, you have more than enough to eat, and you have a roof over your head and

---

32   Romans 1:21
33   Psalm 50

abundance of clothes on your body. Thank Him for His Son, His Spirit, and His Kingdom. Thank Him for the light you have received. Keep going until your perspective begins to change. This is the living edge of spiritual warfare.

I would challenge all of us to take our concordances and search out the words "thanks," "thanksgiving," "thankful," and "thankfulness." It is one of more dominant themes of Scripture but one of the least emphasized as a prime spiritual quality. Thankfulness is like salt, a common and simple thing that changes and enhances the flavor of all it touches.

*4. **Cultivate contentment.*** Contentment is a learned and practiced skill. Paul wrote to the Philippians:

> *I have <u>learned</u> to be content in whatever circumstances I am. I know how to get along with humble means, and I also know how to live in prosperity; in any and every circumstance I have <u>learned</u> the secret of being filled and going hungry, both of having abundance and suffering need. I can do all things through Him who strengthens me.*[34] *[Underline mine]*

Please take careful notice of the context of the overused verse, "I can do all things through Him." The "all things" is specifically *learning to be content* in any and all circumstances. Evidently learning contentment

---

34   Philippians 4:11-13

was difficult enough for Paul that he needed to call upon the strength of Christ to accomplish it!

Contentment implies a state of happy satisfaction. My dear friend and co-laborer for the Kingdom, Darrell Scott[35] writes in his book *Mindfulness* that Psalm 23:1, "I shall not want" does not just refer to having no lack because all my needs are met but also that because the Lord is my shepherd I do not *desire* anything more! This so beautifully catches the implications of Jesus' admonition to not be anxious about life because there is a Father who is watching us and knows our needs before we do. May we now read this Psalm, "Because God is my shepherd I need and desire nothing." It is the picture of contentment.

An important skill in achieving a level of contentment is to carefully distinguish between needs and wants. If we begin to boil our lives down to what we actually *need* we will find that we have a super-abundance of too many things. Paul had learned contentment to such a degree that he was able to tell Timothy, "If we have food and covering, with these we shall be content."[36] Please note that Paul did not require a Lear Jet to accomplish his missionary journeys.

I am not suggesting that to learn contentment we must live in a tent and exist on rice and beans. Rather

35   Darrell Scott is the father of Rachel Joy Scott, the first student to be killed at the Columbine School shooting on April 20, 1999. He is the founder of *Rachel's Challenge* a dynamic organization which is changing lives and reshaping cultures.

36   1 Timothy 6:8

it is adjusting our values to distinguish between wants and needs and learning to be content with those things that genuinely are essential to our functioning in life and in the Kingdom.

5. ***Practice or learn how to be a giver. Remember, it is a skill.*** Because God is the consummate Giver He desires that we will emulate Him. He does not approach His creation with a clinched fist but with an open hand. Other gods ask for sacrifice, either in kind or in actions, but He became the sacrifice on our behalf. Hebrews records the incarnational words of Christ when He says to His Father:

> *Sacrifice and offering you <u>did not desire</u>, but <u>a body you prepared for me</u>; with burnt offerings and sin offerings you were not pleased. Then I said, "Here I am—it is written about me in the scroll—I have <u>come to do your will</u>, O God." [Underline mine]* [37]

Hear Paul as he wrote:

> *He who did not spare His own Son, but delivered Him over for us all, how will He not also with Him freely give us all things?* [38]

How far this departs from the religious image of a God who demands, takes, and withholds. God <u>never requires u</u>s to walk with Him; He *invites* us to

37   Hebrews 10:5-7 (NIV)
38   Romans 8:32

enter into His Kingdom and to come to know Him as Abba. The Father gave the Son, the Son gave Himself, and now they are inviting us to make freely a "self-donation" of ourselves in response to the self-donation that they have made to us. When we begin to see God as a giver we will begin to leave off being takers and enter into the joy of becoming a giver.

Please begin to see yourself as a source of good things freely providing for everyone in your sphere, rather than a consumer. Learn to give for the sheer joy of being a blessing. Herein lies an essential difference between eros and Agape. When eros gives, the open hand continues to be extended waiting for the payoff when something is reciprocated for what has been given. This is exactly the issue Jesus was addressing when He said we should give "in secret" because of the danger of looking for the eros payoff and negating the value of our giving. It is so grievous when people give because "a hundred-fold blessing" has been promised by the preacher in return of their gift. Too often it may be subtly motivated by the eros of greed rather than the Agape of Christ coming from within. I would suggest that whenever you feel pressured or "guilted" into giving an offering, keep your $50 bill in your wallet or purse and give to the family or widow that is barely getting by in life.

We must be shrewd enough to know when we may be injuring others by "helping them get by." By "helping", we may simply be helping them to continue in an addictive life-style or supporting a ne'er-do-well who prefers to live off the hard work of others. True mercy and compassion must empower others to become biblically self-sufficient rather than enabling them to live without responsibility. Please allow the Holy Spirit and good counsel to discern both the predators and the parasites.

6. ***Live by a Kingdom value system.*** I am discovering that there is a value system that most accurately represents the value system by which the Kingdom of God is intended to operate. It very succinctly represents a facet of God's Agape code of conduct, and I think you will quickly agree that if implemented within our society it would radically change the atmosphere from raging division to temperate civility. You may be surprised by simplicity of these three points:

A. I will do what I promise.
B. I will not encroach on that which belongs to others.
C. I am seeking to do good for anyone I can, including you, and if I cannot do good, I will do no harm.

I would love to unfold these more fully, but it would carry us beyond the intended scope of this *Plumbline.* For now, please meditate on these three points. Consider how applying them might transform your actions and relationships.

*7. **Govern your possessions (especially finances); do not allow them to govern you.*** We now return to where we started. Will possessions and money be your god, or will you govern them as Kingdom citizens? Other than cultivating the disciplines we have already explored, allow me to suggest some simple practices that will bring you freedom and joy if implemented.

Get out of debt and stay out. Other than things that you must have in order to live, a home, an automobile, endeavor to save until you are able to afford something. If you must finance an automobile, be wise enough to purchase a Chevrolet rather than a Cadillac. Heed the wisdom of Ray Dalio, a secular billionaire:

> *Buying something you can't afford means spending more than you make. You're not just borrowing from your lender; you are borrowing from your future self. Essentially, you are creating a time in the future in which you will need to spend less than you make so you can pay it back. The pattern of borrowing, spending more than you make, and then having to spend less than you make very quickly resembles a cycle. This is as true for a national economy as it is for an individual. Borrowing money sets a mechanical, predictable series of events into motion.*

It is not easy, but we can learn to discern between needs and wants. Resist impulse buying. A wise man once said that if you desire to buy something, wait three days and see if it is as important as it seemed at the time and whether or not you really need it. Check your hidden motives. Is your planned purchase to make you feel better or look better rather than yielding more economy and efficiency?

Save! I know this seems impossible when you are living close to the margins, but even a few dollars put aside on a regular basis and saved for necessary or unexpected expenses can provide a cushion against further debt and hardship. If money is committed to saving immediately it becomes unavailable for discretionary spending, and you will learn to live on less.

Make a budget. Everyone likes to object that their paychecks are so tightly committed that making a budget is an exercise in futility. Be that as it may, once our spending is on paper it allows for the possibility of the wisdom of God to be applied in creative and surprising ways.

CONCLUSION:

Please do not religiously over react about money and embrace poverty and lack as something inherently spiritual. For many years I labored under a fear of prospering because I so feared the destruction into which I had seen many wonderful servants of God fall because they succumbed to the song of the other god. I have found that this attitude of resisting the abundance of God's blessing can be as detrimental to the ultimate purposes the Kingdom as avarice. Wealth can be a powerful means of advancing the gospel and extending the compassion of Christ into a hurting world. It is not the amount that is important—it is the attitude and motivation.

I do not believe it is coincidental that many of Jesus' parables dealt with money. He understood that the ability to govern the power of mammon demonstrated the ability to handle greater responsibility. In many ways how we handle money and possessions is a litmus test of maturity and may be a qualifying factor for promotion in the Kingdom of God. Unfortunately, this skill has been mentored little in the church. Those in ministry and those who function in secular life must learn to engage the world in Agape rather than with eros and greed. May Father grant us to become genuine givers rather than takers and to engage the world as shrewd sheep rather than hungry wolves.

LIFECHANGERS®

P.O. Box 3709 ❖ Cookeville, TN 38502
931.520.3730 ❖ lc@lifechangers.org

www.ingramcontent.com/pod-product-compliance
Lightning Source LLC
Chambersburg PA
CBHW060043040426
42331CB00032B/2259